CAST IRON COOKBOOK

Easy Cast Iron Skillet Home Cooking Recipes

(Classic and Modern Recipes for Your Lodge Cast Iron Cookware)

Kenneth Wood

Published by Sharon Lohan

© Kenneth Wood

All Rights Reserved

Cast Iron Cookbook: Easy Cast Iron Skillet Home Cooking Recipes (Classic and Modern Recipes for Your Lodge Cast Iron Cookware)

ISBN 978-1-990334-96-2

All rights reserved. No part of this guide may be reproduced in any form without permission in writing from the publisher except in the case of brief quotations embodied in critical articles or reviews.

Legal & Disclaimer

The information contained in this book is not designed to replace or take the place of any form of medicine or professional medical advice. The information in this book has been provided for educational and entertainment purposes only.

The information contained in this book has been compiled from sources deemed reliable, and it is accurate to the best of the Author's knowledge; however, the Author cannot guarantee its accuracy and validity and cannot be held liable for any errors or omissions. Changes are periodically made to this book. You must consult your doctor or get professional medical advice before using any of the suggested remedies, techniques, or information in this book.

Table of contents

Part 1 1

Introduction 2

1. Taco Ring 3

2. Baked Berry Oatmeal 5

3. Skillet Fried Eggs 7

4. Sourdough French Toast With Baked Pears 9

5. Cheesy Red Potato & Garlic Scape Hash 11

6. Potato & Rosemary Frittata 13

7. Sausage & Cheddar Breakfast Casserole 15

8. Candied Bacon 17

9. Chocolate Chip & Walnut Banana Bread 19

10. Monkey Bread 21

11. No-Knead Dutch Oven Bread 24

12. Garlic Smashed Potatoes 26

13. Chocolate Omelet Soufflé 28

14. German-Style Apple Pancake (Pfannkuchen) 30

15. Mexican Mac And Cheese 32

16. Spicy Baked Beans 34

17. Brussels Sprouts In Olive Oil With Pistachios 36

18. Brown Butter Sweet Carrots 38

19. Fried Plantains With Cinnamon & Honey 40

20. Sweet And Tangy Glazed Carrots With Cranberries 42

21. Spanish Quesadillas 44

22. Slow Roasted Root Vegetables.................................... 46

23. Seared Scallops... 48

24. Blackened Red Drum.. 50

25. Glazed Butternut Squash.. 52

26. Cheesy Stone-Ground Grits 54

27. Savory Mushroom, Spinach, And Feta Bread Pudding...... 56

28. Ginger-Spice-Topped Peach Cobbler 59

29. Raspberry-Blackberry Crisp 62

30. Roast Chicken With Root Vegetables 64

Conclusion.. 66

Part 2.. 67

Recipe 1: Simple Cheesy Omelet...................................... 68

Recipe 2: Cast Iron Style Chicken Piccata........................ 70

Recipe 3: Cast Iron Skillet Baked Chocolate Chip Cookie 72

Recipe 4: Spicy Cast Iron Salsa 74

Recipe 5: Indoor Style S'mores... 76

Recipe 6: Ginger And Peach Shortbread Cobbler 77

Recipe 7: Sweet Tasting Blueberry Cobbler..................... 79

Recipe 8: Sweet Tasting Potato And Green Onion Cakes......... 81

Recipe 9: Classic Artichoke And Kale Dip........................ 83

Recipe 10: Tasty Chicken And Wild Rice......................... 85

Recipe 11: Four Cheese Rigatoni 88

Recipe 12: Cast Iron Mac And Cheese 91

Recipe 13: Tasty Blue Cheese And Beet Risotto 93

Recipe 14: Cast Iron Filet Mignon 95

Recipe 15: Cast Iron Bbq Style Pizza 96

Recipe 16: Pecan Okra 98

Recipe 17: Lamb Chops In Garlic Mint Sauce 100

Recipe 18: Simple Cowboy Style Steak 102

Recipe 19: Easy Egg And Sweet Potato Skillet 104

Recipe 20: Simple Cast Iron Lasagna 106

Recipe 21: Simple Cast Iron Fried Chicken 108

Recipe 22: Simple Cast Iron Pizza 110

Part 1

Introduction

Looking for simple, beginner-friendly cast iron recipes? If so, you're in the right place. This book contains a variety of sweet and savory recipes that can be made either in a cast iron skillet or Dutch oven. From breakfast recipes like baked berry oatmeal and potato and rosemary frittata to desserts like banana bread and chocolate omelet, this book covers almost every area.

Almost all the recipes in this book are easy and beginner-friendly. With basic ingredients and detailed instructions, you'll be whipping up delicious dishes in no time. Let's begin!

1. Taco Ring

A simple taco roll ring recipe that serves great as a party snack or appetizer.

Makes: 6-8 servings

Prep: 20 mins

Cook: 45 mins

Ingredients:

- 1 tube crescent roll dough
- ½ lb. ground beef, browned and drained
- ¾ cup shredded taco blend cheese
- ¼ cup salsa
- ¼ cup sliced jalapeno
- ½ cup shredded lettuce
- ½ cup sour cream

Directions:

Lightly grease a 10" pie plate with vegetable shortening. Unroll and separate the crescent rolls.

Arrange the crescent rolls around the perimeter of the pie plate, each pointing out, making a sunburst shape. With the backs of your fingers, slightly flatten the overlapping pieces of crescent dough.

Spoon the browned ground beef on the crescent dough, being careful not to cover the outer and inner edges of dough. Top with the shredded cheese.

Take each outer point of crescent dough and pull it toward the center, partly covering the ground beef filling. Press the tips firmly into the center portion of dough to seal. There will be gaps between each strip of dough.

Place pie plate in a shallow 12" cast iron Dutch oven with feet and cover with flat lid. Arrange 6 hot coals in a circle and place Dutch oven directly above hot coals. Add 8-10 more hot coals around perimeter of lid. Bake, without lifting lid, for 45 minutes, adding additional hot coals after first 30 minutes.

To serve, carefully remove pie plate from Dutch oven with oven gloves. Cut into wedges and serve with salsa, jalapeno, lettuce and sour cream.

2. Baked Berry Oatmeal

Baked oatmeal is a wonderful breakfast—it's sweet, filling, and endlessly adaptable.

Makes: 4 servings

Prep: 5 mins

Cook: 45 mins

Ingredients:

- 2 cups rolled oats
- 1 cup fresh blueberries
- 1 cup fresh strawberries, halved
- ½ cup chopped pecans
- 1 tablespoon packed brown sugar
- 1 teaspoon ground cinnamon
- 1 teaspoon baking powder
- ½ teaspoon sea salt
- 2 eggs
- 1½ cups whole milk

- ¼ cup honey
- 3 tablespoons salted butter, melted

Directions:

Preheat the oven to 350°F.

In a large bowl, mix the oats, blueberries, strawberries, pecans, brown sugar, cinnamon, baking powder, and sea salt.

In a med. bowl, whisk the eggs, milk, honey, and butter. Fold the milk mixture into the oat mixture. Spoon the batter into the skillet.

Bake for 40-45 mins., or until crisp around the edges and cooked through. Serve hot.

SERVING TIP: Serve topped with crème fraîche or yogurt for a deliciously quick breakfast.

3. Skillet Fried Eggs

With a pat of butter (about 1 tablespoon) and a well-seasoned cast iron skillet, you're mere minutes away from the perfect fried egg.

Makes: 1 serving

Prep: 3 mins

Cook: 5-7 mins

Ingredients:

- 1 egg
- 1 tablespoon salted butter
- Pinch sea salt

Directions:

In the skillet over med-high heat, melt the butter.

Crack the egg into the skillet, on the hottest part of the skillet. Sprinkle the yolk with the sea salt.

Watch the egg carefully.

•For an over-easy egg: When the white has cooked through, after about 4 minutes, flip the egg while the yolk is still liquid. Cook for 1 minute and serve.

•For an over-medium egg: When the rim of the yolk has cooked through, after about 5 mins, flip the egg and cook for 1 min before serving.

•For an over-well egg: When the yolk has almost completely cooked through, after about 6 mins, flip the egg and cook for 1 min and serve.

4. Sourdough French Toast With Baked Pears

The beauty of French toast is that it is s a delicious base for many toppings. Use your imagination and experiment!

Makes: 4 servings

Prep: 10 mins

Cook: 25 mins

Ingredients:

For the baked pears:

- 2 pears, quartered and cored
- 4 tablespoons salted butter, cubed
- 1 teaspoon ground cinnamon

For the French toast:

- 4 eggs
- ½ cup whole milk
- 1 tablespoon sugar
- 1 teaspoon vanilla extract
- 1 teaspoon ground cinnamon
- 1 teaspoon ground ginger

- 4 tablespoons salted butter
- 1 loaf crusty sourdough bread, cut into ¾- to 1-inch slices
- Honey, for serving

Directions:

To make the pears:

Preheat the oven to 350°F.

Place the pears in the skillet, top with the butter cubes and cinnamon, and bake for 25 minutes.

To make the French toast:

In a large, shallow bowl, whisk the 4 eggs, sugar, milk, cinnamon, vanilla and ginger.

Preheat the griddle over medium-high heat. Add 1 tablespoon of butter to melt.

Place a piece of bread in the cinnamon and egg mixture, submerging it completely and turning it for a full coating. Place in the hot skillet. Stir the batter before dunking each slice to ensure that the spices stay evenly distributed. Repeat with the remaining slices and the remaining butter and egg mixture.

Cook the bread for 2 to 3 minutes per side until crisp and browned. Keep the French toast warm in the microwave or covered loosely with a clean kitchen towel.

Serve warm, topped with the baked pears and a drizzle of honey.

5. Cheesy Red Potato & Garlic Scape Hash

A garlic-filled potato and cheese hash recipe. Great for breakfast, lunch or dinner.

Makes: 4 servings

Prep: 20 mins

Cook: 15 mins

Ingredients:

- 2 tablespoons salted butter
- 3 garlic cloves, minced
- 1 white onion, chopped
- Sea salt
- Freshly ground black pepper
- 6 to 8 small red potatoes, grated
- ¼ pound Cheddar cheese, grated
- 5 to 6 garlic scapes or scallions (white and light green parts), minced

Directions:

In the skillet over medium heat, melt the butter

Add the garlic and onion. Season with sea salt and black pepper. Stir to combine.

Stir in the potatoes to mix thoroughly. Cook for about 15 minutes, stirring every 2 to 3 minutes, until the potatoes are cooked.

Remove stir in the Cheddar cheese. Sprinkle with garlic scapes. Serve hot.

6. Potato & Rosemary Frittata

A frittata—somewhere between an omelet, a torta, and a quiche—is well suited to cooking in a cast iron skillet because the even distribution of heat in the oven cooks the eggs nicely.

Makes: 6 servings

Prep: 15 mins

Cook: 30 mins

Ingredients:

- 2 tablespoons salted butter
- 1 large red potato, thinly sliced
- 1 yellow onion, chopped
- 2 garlic cloves, minced
- 6 eggs
- ½ cup shredded Cheddar cheese
- 4 tbsp. water
- 2 tablespoons fresh rosemary leaves, chopped
- Pinch sea salt

Directions:

Preheat the oven to 350°F.

In the skillet, melt the butter over medium heat. Add the potato, onion, and garlic, and cook for about 10 minutes, stirring occasionally, until the potato begins to soften. Spread the mix at the base of the skillet.

In a large bowl, whisk the eggs, cheese, water, rosemary, and sea salt. Pour the egg over the potato mixture in the skillet. Cook for 3 to 5 minutes, or until the eggs begin to set. Transfer the skillet to the oven.

Bake for 12-15 mins. Slice in wedges and serve hot.

7. Sausage & Cheddar Breakfast Casserole

A hot, cheesy, spicy dish that is perfect for Christmas morning.

Makes: 6 servings

Prep: 15 mins

Cook: 1 hr. 15 mins

Ingredients:

- 8 eggs
- 1½ cups whole milk
- 1 teaspoon dry mustard
- 1 teaspoon ground paprika
- 1 teaspoon red pepper flakes
- 1 teaspoon sea salt
- 1 tablespoon salted butter
- 1 pound ground sausage
- 1 white onion, diced
- 2 garlic cloves, minced

- 4 cups cubed bread
- 1 cup shredded Cheddar cheese

Directions:

Preheat the oven to 375°F.

In a bowl, whisk the mustard, milk, eggs, paprika, red pepper flakes, and sea salt.

In a cast-iron skillet over medium heat, melt the butter.

Add the sausage and cook for 8 -10 mins, stirring frequently, until almost cooked through.

Stir in the onion and garlic. Sauté for 3 to 4 minutes, until the onions are tender and the sausage is fully cooked. Remove from the heat.

Add the bread cubes and Cheddar cheese to the skillet and toss to combine.

Pour the egg mixture over the top.

Bake for 50-60 mins, or until cooked and puffed.

8. Candied Bacon

A spiced candied bacon side dish that is absolutely to die for.

Makes: 4 servings

Prep: 5 mins

Cook: 20-30 mins

Ingredients:

- ½ cup packed dark brown sugar
- 1 tablespoon ground cinnamon
- 1 teaspoon ground ginger
- 1 teaspoon ground cloves
- 1 tablespoon salted butter
- 1 pound thick-cut bacon

Directions:

In a bowl, mix together the sugar & the spices.

In the skillet over med. heat, melt the butter.

Add each piece of bacon in spiced sugar and add to the skillet. Do not overcrowd the skillet. Fry the bacon for 4-5 mins. per side until crisp. Transfer to a wire rack to drain. Repeat until all the bacon is cooked.

9. Chocolate Chip & Walnut Banana Bread

With a combination of spices, chopped nuts, chocolate chips, and those bananas, this bread is dense, sweet, and nutty.

Makes: 6-8 servings

Prep: 20 mins

Cook: 1 hr.

Ingredients:

- 2 eggs
- ½ cup sugar
- 3 ripe bananas, diced
- 1 teaspoon ground nutmeg
- 1 teaspoon ground cinnamon
- ½ cup buttermilk
- ½ cup honey
- 1 teaspoon vanilla extract

- ½ cup chopped walnuts
- ½ cup dark chocolate chips
- 2 cups all-purpose flour
- 1 tablespoon salted butter

Directions:

Preheat the oven to 400°F.

In a bowl, mix together the 2 eggs and sugar.

Fold in the bananas, nutmeg, and cinnamon.

Stir in the buttermilk, honey, vanilla, walnuts, and chocolate chips.

Mix in the flour, ½ cup at a time, until it is completely incorporated.

Grease the skillet with the butter and pour the batter into it.

Bake for 50 to 60 minutes, or until the top is firm when gently pressed and nicely browned.

10. Monkey Bread

A delicious, warm, gooey, sweet, monkey bread recipe with spiced caramel glaze.

Makes: 4-6 servings

Prep: 2 ½ hrs.

Cook: 25 mins

Ingredients:

For the sugar coating:

- 1 cup packed dark brown sugar
- 2 teaspoons ground cinnamon
- ½ cup (1 stick) salted butter, melted

For the dough:

- Olive oil, for the bowl
- 1 cup whole milk
- 2 tablespoons granulated sugar
- 2 tablespoons shortening

- 1 teaspoon sea salt
- ¼ cup warm water
- 1 tablespoon active dry yeast
- 1 egg, beaten
- 2½ cups bread flour

For the glaze:

- 4 tbsp. salted butter
- ½ cup packed dark brown sugar
- ¼ cup honey
- 1 tablespoon water
- 1 teaspoon ground cinnamon
- 1 teaspoon ground ginger

Directions:

To make the sugar coating:

In a small bowl, mix the dark brown sugar, cinnamon, and melted butter, and set aside.

To make the dough:

Grease a bowl with a little olive oil and set aside.

In a medium saucepan over med-high heat, scald the milk by bringing it almost to a boil and then remove. Stir in the granulated sugar, shortening, and sea salt, stir until the sugar and shortening melt, and let cool until lukewarm.

In a small bowl, whisk the water and yeast until the yeast dissolves. Stir the yeast into the milk mixture.

Add the egg and stir to combine.

Stir the flour into the yeast mixture, ½ cup at a time, until it forms a soft dough. Place the dough out onto a slightly floured surface (or a silicone baking mat), adding more flour as necessary to prevent it from getting tacky, and knead for 10 minutes. Transfer the dough to the oiled bowl, cover loosely with a clean kitchen towel, and let rise for 1 hour.

Place the dough out onto a slightly floured surface (or a silicone baking mat) and roll it into a 12-by-16-inch rectangle, ¼ inch thick. Cut the dough into 48 2-by-2-inch squares. Roll each into a ball, dunk each into the sugar coating, covering completely, and place in the Dutch oven. Place a kitchen towel let it rise for 1 hour.

Preheat the oven to 350°F. Bake the bread for 25 minutes. Cover with foil and bake for 1/2 an hour.

To make the glaze:

While the monkey bread bakes, in a small saucepan over low heat, warm the butter, dark brown sugar, honey, water, cinnamon, and ginger, stirring frequently.

When the monkey bread comes out of the oven, pour the glaze evenly over it and let sit for 10 minutes. Serve warm.

11. No-Knead Dutch Oven Bread

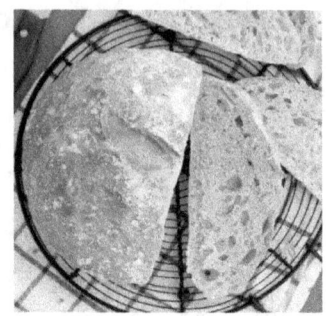

The key to a successful no-knead bread is time. Left for 12 hours to rise, the dough slowly ferments, and the result is crispy and crunchy on the outside and warm, soft and delicious on the inside.

Makes: 4-6 servings

Prep: 15 mins

Inactive Time: 12 hrs.

Cook: 45 mins

Ingredients:

- 2 tbsp. olive oil, plus more for the bowl
- 4 cups all-purpose flour
- 2 teaspoons sea salt
- 1 teaspoon active dry yeast
- 2 cups warm water

Directions:

Grease a bowl with a little olive oil & set aside.

In another large bowl, mix the flour, sea salt, and yeast.

Pour the warm water over the flour mixture and stir well to incorporate. Transfer the dough to the oiled bowl, cover loosely with a clean kitchen towel, and let rise for 12 hours or overnight.

Preheat the oven to 450°F.

Put the Dutch oven in.

Transfer the dough to the warmed Dutch oven. Cover the pot and return it to the oven for 40 minutes.

Remove the lid and bake for 15 minutes, until browned on top and baked through.

Let cool before slicing and serving warm.

VARIATION TIP: Mix 2 tablespoons of fresh herbs, such as rosemary leaves, thyme, or oregano, into the dough for an easy herbed bread.

12. Garlic Smashed Potatoes

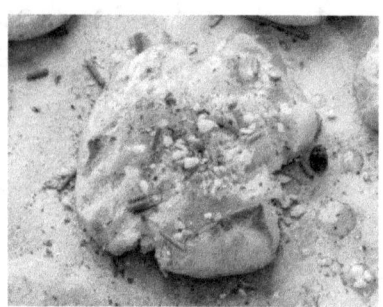

Smashed potatoes combine everything that is great about mashed potatoes with everything that is great about roasted potatoes.

Makes: 4 servings

Prep: 10 mins

Cook: 1 hr. 15 mins

Ingredients:

- 7 to 10 small or medium red potatoes
- ¼ cup olive oil, divided
- 1 teaspoon sea salt, divided
- 1 teaspoon red pepper flakes, divided
- Freshly ground black pepper
- 4 tablespoons salted butter, cubed
- 3 garlic cloves, minced

Directions:

Preheat the oven to 350°F.

In the skillet, toss the potatoes with 2 tablespoons of olive oil, ½ teaspoon of sea salt, ½ tsp of red pepper flakes, and a pinch of black pepper.

Roast for 30 minutes, or until a fork easily penetrates the potatoes.

Increase the oven temperature to 425°F.

With a potato masher, smash the potatoes flat. Return to the oven and roast for 25 minutes.

Flip the potatoes, and top with the remaining 2 tablespoons of olive oil, the butter cubes, the remaining ½ teaspoon of sea salt, the remaining ½ teaspoon of red pepper flakes, a pinch of black pepper, and the garlic. Roast for 15-20 mins, until cooked through, brown, and crisp.

13. Chocolate Omelet Soufflé

If you are a chocoholic who loves simple yet intensely rich indulgences, then this dessert is a real treat and easy to make.

Makes: 4 servings

Prep: 10 mins

Cook: 15 mins

Ingredients:

- ¼ cup coarsely chopped walnut pieces
- 1 teaspoon vanilla
- 8 ounces semisweet chocolate, melted
- 4 large eggs
- ⅓ cup heavy cream
- 3 Tablespoons clarified butter
- 3 Tablespoons confectioners' sugar
- Sweetened whipped cream, to garnish

Directions:

Preheat your oven to 425°F. Toss the walnuts with the vanilla. Place them on a baking sheet with aluminum foil and bake in the oven for 5 to 6 minutes, watching that they don't burn.

In a bowl, beat the eggs and cream to blend; add the melted chocolate and beat vigorously until frothy.

Heat a 10-inch cast iron skillet over med. heat until just hot, about 3 minutes; add the butter and walnuts, and cook for 30 seconds. Pour in the egg-chocolate mixture and cook for 1 minute. Put the skillet to the oven and bake until slightly firm, 8 to 9 minutes. Remove from the oven, and immediately invert the omelet onto a 10-inch plate. Dust with confectioners' sugar and cut in wedges, serving each portion with a generous dollop of whipped cream.

14. German-Style Apple Pancake (Pfannkuchen)

Puffy German apple pancakes with icing sugar on top. The perfect way to start any day.

Makes: 4 servings

Prep: 10 mins

Cook: 30 mins

Ingredients:

- 1 large tart-sweet apple, such as Cortland, peeled, cored, and thinly sliced
- Juice and zest of 1 lemon
- 4 large eggs, separated
- ½ cup whole milk
- 2 Tablespoons sugar
- 2 Tablespoons cornstarch
- ½ teaspoon salt
- 2 Tablespoons unsalted butter
- Confectioners' sugar, to garnish

Directions:

Preheat your oven to 400°F. Heat a 10-inch cast-iron skillet over med. heat until hot, about 3 minutes.

In a bowl, combine the apples with 1 tbsp. of the lemon juice and set aside. In a bowl, beat together the yolks, milk, sugar, cornstarch, salt, and lemon zest. In a bowl, whisk the egg whites into soft peaks. Using a flexible spatula, gently fold the yolks into the whites until just mixed.

Add the butter to the heated skillet. When the butter foams, add the apples, turning to coat them with butter, and then arrange them in a single layer. Pour the egg mixture over the slices of apples. Partially cover and cook for 10 minutes. Uncover the skillet, transfer it to the oven, and bake for about 15 minutes, or until the bottom of the pfannkuchen is nicely browned and it is set in the middle.

Remove, sprinkle with the confectioners' sugar and remaining lemon juice, and serve immediately.

15. Mexican Mac And Cheese

Classic mac and cheese takes a south-of-the-border turn with the addition of a chipotle in adobo, which imparts a hint of heat, and the crushed tortillas and Cotija cheese used for the topping.

Makes: 6 servings

Prep: 10 mins

Cook: 40 mins

Ingredients:

- Salt
- 8 ounces uncooked wagon wheel macaroni
- 2 Tablespoons unsalted butter
- ¾ cup finely chopped onion
- ½ tablespoon minced garlic
- 1 teaspoon ground cumin
- ½ teaspoon ground coriander
- 2 Tablespoons all-purpose flour

- 2 cups milk
- 1 chipotle en adobo, minced
- ½ cup sundried tomatoes, thinly sliced
- 2 ¼ cups grated sharp Cheddar cheese
- 1 cup grated Jack cheese
- 1 ½ cups crushed tortilla chips
- 1 1/3 cups freshly grated Cotija cheese

Directions:

Cook the pasta according to package directions. Remove, drain, and set aside.

Heat a 10-inch cast-iron skillet over med. heat until hot. Add the butter, onion, garlic, cumin, and coriander, and cook over medium-low heat, stirring often, until the onion is softened, about 7 minutes.

Preheat your oven to 350°F.

Add the flour to the softened onions and stir continuously for 3 minutes. Whisk in the milk and bring to a boil. Reduce & simmer for 2 minutes. Add the chipotle and tomatoes and cool slightly; add the cheeses and stir until melted. Stir the pasta into the cheese mixture.

In a bowl, toss the tortilla chips and Cotija cheese together and drizzle on top of the macaroni. Bake until the dish is hot and the top is golden brown, 25 to 30 minutes. Serve.

16. Spicy Baked Beans

If you're a fan of baked beans with a little heat, this simple version—emboldened with chipotle chilies in adobo sauce—will assuredly excite your taste buds.

Makes: 12 servings

Prep: 10 mins

Cook: 5 hrs.

Ingredients:

- 2 pounds pea or navy beans, rinsed and picked over
- 1 Tablespoon salt or to taste
- 2 Tablespoons vegetable oil
- 1 ½ cups chopped yellow onions
- 2 chipotle chilies in adobo sauce, chopped
- ⅓ cup Dijon mustard
- ⅓ cup firmly packed dark brown sugar
- 1 (18-ounce) jar high-quality smoky barbecue sauce
- Boiling water

Directions:

Put the beans in a large cast-iron Dutch oven with enough water to cover. Bring to a boil and cook for 3 minutes; turn off the heat, cover, and let them stand for 1 hour. Drain, and then cover again with water, add salt, and bring to a boil for 5 mins, lower heat cover, and cook for 30 mins more. Remove from the heat, pour the beans and their liquid into a large bowl, and let them stand in the liquid until cooled.

Meanwhile, preheat your oven to 250°F.

Heat a Dutch oven over medium-high heat until hot. Add the oil and onions and sauté until golden brown, 3 to 4 minutes.

Drain the beans and add in the onions, chipotle chilies, mustard, brown sugar, and barbecue sauce. Add boiling hot water to just cover the beans, cover the pot, and bake for 4 hours. Remove the top for the last 30 mins of cooking time, or until the liquid is reduced and the beans are very tender. Let them stand for 15 mins before serving.

17. Brussels Sprouts In Olive Oil With Pistachios

This delicious recipe will delight even Brussel sprouts haters. The Brussels sprouts are blanched in salted water to keep them bright green, then finished with pistachios.

Makes: 4 servings

Prep: 5 mins

Cook: 5 mins

Ingredients:

- 1 pound Brussels sprouts, outer leaves removed, cored and quartered lengthwise
- Kosher salt
- 1 ½ Tablespoons olive or vegetable oil
- Leaves from 2 sprigs fresh thyme, chopped
- ¼ cup (2 ounces) shelled pistachios
- Freshly ground black pepper

Directions:

Bring a large pan or a pot of salted water to a boil. Place the sprouts in & cook for 3 mins. Drain, rinse the sprouts using cold water, and then dry on a clean towel.

Add the oil, thyme, Brussels sprouts, and pistachios to a large cast-iron skillet and cook until heated through, turning often. Season to taste and then serve.

18. Brown Butter Sweet Carrots

Slow cooked in butter and brown sugar, these carrots are seriously addictive.

Makes: 4-6 servings

Prep: 15 mins

Cook: 55 mins

Ingredients:

- ½ pound thick-cut bacon, chopped
- 4 tablespoons salted butter
- 12 to 15 large carrots, cut into ½-inch slices
- ¼ cup packed brown sugar
- 2 garlic cloves, minced
- Pinch sea salt
- Pinch red pepper flakes

Directions:

In the skillet over medium-low heat, combine the bacon and butter. Cook for about 10 minutes, stirring frequently, until the bacon browns slightly.

Add the carrots, brown sugar, garlic, sea salt, and red pepper flakes. Stir to coat the carrots thoroughly with bacon drippings and butter.

Simmer, uncovered, for 45 minutes, stirring occasionally, or until the carrots soften but are still firm.

19. Fried Plantains With Cinnamon & Honey

Fried plantains will quickly become a favorite treat because they are quick, easy, and intensely satisfying.

Makes: 4 servings

Prep: 5 mins

Cook: 10 mins

Ingredients:

- 2 ripe plantains, cut ½ inch thick
- 1 teaspoon ground cinnamon
- 2 tablespoons salted butter
- ¼ cup honey

Directions:

In a medium bowl, put the plantains and sprinkle them with cinnamon.

On a cast iron griddle over medium-high heat, melt the butter.

Add the plantains and cook for 3 to 4 minutes per side.

Serve hot with the honey to dip.

SERVING TIP: Serve with chocolate gelato instead of honey for a doubly delicious dessert.

20. Sweet And Tangy Glazed Carrots With Cranberries

When honey and vinegar plus a handful of dried cranberries are reduced to glaze young carrots, it becomes a memorable side dish to enjoy for holidays or anytime you want a special vegetable.

Makes: 4 servings

Prep: 10 mins

Cook: 30 mins

Ingredients:

- 1 ½ pounds young carrots, peeled or large carrots cut lengthwise into quarters and in half widthwise
- 1 Tablespoon canola or vegetable oil
- 1 teaspoon salt
- ½ cup good-quality vegetable stock
- 1 Tablespoon unsalted butter
- ¼ cup dried cranberries
- 2 Tablespoons thyme honey or other variety

- 2 Tablespoons sherry or white wine vinegar
- 1 Tablespoon finely chopped flat-leaf parsley

Directions:

Combine the salt, oil, and carrots in a bowl. Heat a cast-iron skillet over med. heat until just hot, about 3 ½ minutes. Scrape the carrots into the pan oil and cook for 2 minutes, stirring once or twice. Stir in the stock and butter, cover the skillet, reduce the heat to low, and cook for 15 mins.

Remove the lid and stir in the vinegar, honey, and cranberries. Bring to a boil and cook until the liquid reduces to glaze the carrots, about 5 minutes, shaking the pan occasionally. Stir in the parsley and serve.

21. Spanish Quesadillas

These tasty triangles are filled with Spanish ingredients—Manchego cheese and jalapeños—and topped with Spanish smoked paprika.

Makes: 8 triangles

Prep: 10 mins

Cook: 10 mins

Ingredients:

- 3 jalapeños
- 1 cup (4 ounces) shredded Manchego cheese
- 2 (10-inch) flour tortillas
- Olive oil
- 1/2 Tablespoon small capers, blotted dry
- Pinch of sweet Pimentón de la Vera

Directions:

Heat a cast-iron skillet over medium heat. Add the jalapeños and roast until the skins are blackened. Place roasted jalapeños into a plastic bag until cool enough to handle, then remove the skins and chop.

Sprinkle 1/2 of the cheese evenly over one tortilla and cover with the jalapeños. Sprinkle on the capers, then cover with the remaining cheese and second tortilla.

Heat a 10-inch cast-iron skillet over med. heat until hot, 3 ½ to 4 minutes; brush with a little oil. Put the filled quesadilla in the pan, brush the top with a little oil, and put a small skillet or pan on top and cook until the edges of the tortilla are browned, 2 to 3 minutes. With a wide spatula, flip the tortilla, and cook the other side until lightly browned, about 2 minutes. Remove the quesadilla, sprinkle on the Pimentón de la Vera, and let it stand for 1 minute; then cut into eighths with a pizza cutter or sharp knife and serve.

22. Slow Roasted Root Vegetables

Delicious root veggies with garlic and rosemary.

Makes: 6 servings

Prep: 10 mins

Cook: 75-90 mins

Ingredients:

- 1 bag baby carrots
- 2 onions, peeled and cut in wedges
- 3 parsnips, peeled and cut into thick slices
- 1 lb. baby red potatoes, washed
- 6 cloves whole garlic, peeled
- 3 Tbs. olive oil
- ½ tsp. sea salt
- ½ tsp. ground black pepper
- ¼ tsp. dried rosemary

Directions:

In a 12" cast iron Dutch oven with feet, combine vegetables and garlic cloves. Drizzle with olive oil and mix to coat evenly. Add salt, pepper and rosemary. Gently mix together.

Arrange 4 hot coals in a circle and place Dutch oven over coals. Cover with flat lid and top with 6 more hot coals. Let roast for 75-90 minutes, adding fresh coals as needed.

Serve hot.

23. Seared Scallops

Almost nothing tastes better than a fresh scallop quickly seared in butter, so this recipe keeps it simple. Salt, butter, lemon juice, and a hot skillet.

Makes: 4 servings

Prep: 5 mins

Cook: 5 mins

Ingredients:

- 3 tablespoons salted butter
- 1 dozen sea scallops, rinsed and patted dry
- Pinch sea salt
- Juice of 1 lemon

Directions:

Place a cast iron skillet over medium-high heat.

Add the butter to melt.

Place the scallops in the skillet. Sprinkle with sea salt and cook for 2 minutes. Flip and cook the other side for 2 minutes.

Remove the scallops from the heat, sprinkle with the lemon juice, and serve.

24. Blackened Red Drum

Drum is a firm fish with a moderate flavor and is particularly delicious when blackened.

Makes: 4 servings

Prep: 10 mins

Cook: 10 mins

Ingredients:

- 1 teaspoon ground chipotle chili pepper
- 1 teaspoon dried oregano
- 1 teaspoon freshly ground black pepper
- 1 teaspoon sea salt
- ½ teaspoon cayenne pepper
- ¼ teaspoon red pepper flakes
- 4 red drum fillets, skinned and boned
- 4 tablespoons salted butter, melted
- Juice of 1 lemon

Directions:

In a bowl, stir together the chipotle pepper, oregano, black pepper, sea salt, cayenne pepper, and red pepper flakes. Set aside.

Place a dry cast iron skillet over medium-high heat.

Brush each fillet on both sides with melted butter and carefully coat both sides with the spice mixture.

Add the fillets to the hot skillet and cook for 2 to 3 minutes per side, until blackened and cooked through.

Drizzle with lemon juice and serve.

25. Glazed Butternut Squash

Butternut squash, luxuriously glazed with brown sugar, maple syrup, and bourbon, is so delicious, you may find everyone asking for seconds.

Makes: 4-6 servings

Prep: 10 mins

Cook: 20 mins

Ingredients:

- 1 ¼ pounds peeled butternut squash, cut into 1-inch chunks
- 1 Tablespoon canola or vegetable oil
- Salt and freshly ground black pepper
- 2 Tablespoons unsalted butter
- 2 Tablespoons firmly packed dark brown sugar
- 2 Tablespoons light amber maple syrup
- 2 Tablespoons bourbon
- 2 teaspoons minced fresh rosemary leaves (optional)

Directions:

Toss the squash with the oil, about 1 teaspoon of salt, and pepper to taste. Heat a 10-inch cast-iron skillet over med-high heat, 3 ½ to 4minutes. Add the squash and cook until lightly browned on all sides, about 5 minutes, turning often.

Add the maple syrup, brown sugar, and butter; bring to a boil, and cook until the sugar is melted, turning to coat the squash. Off the heat, carefully pour in the bourbon (it might flame) and cook until the flames subside. Cover and cook over med. heat until the squash is almost tender, about 10 minutes, then uncover and gently reduce the liquid until it glazes the squash, about 3 minutes more, turning often. Stir in the rosemary, if using, and serve.

26. Cheesy Stone-Ground Grits

If you haven't tried slowly simmered grits, liberally laced with Cheddar cheese, you're in for a treat.

Makes: 6 servings

Prep: 10 mins

Cook: 1-2 hrs.

Ingredients:

- 2+ cups vegetable stock
- 2 cups whole milk
- 1 cup coarse stone-ground grits, preferably white
- 1 Tablespoon unsalted butter
- 2 cups (8 oz.) shredded sharp white Cheddar cheese
- Salt
- Tabasco or other hot sauce (optional)

Directions:

Combine 2 cups of stock and the milk in a 10-inch cast-iron Dutch oven and bring a boil. Add the grits, stirring continuously until blended and smooth. Lower and then simmer according to the package directions until the grits are tender, about 1 hour (some brands can take up to 2 hours), stirring frequently.

If the mixture gets thick and starts to dry out, stir in more liquid—water or stock by ¼-cupfuls—until smooth. Once the grits are cooked, add in the butter and cheese and cook until melted. Season to taste with salt and Tabasco sauce, if desired, before serving.

27. Savory Mushroom, Spinach, And Feta Bread Pudding

This simple-to-make bread pudding makes a sophisticated centerpiece for brunch, lunch, or on a buffet. Serve it with a green salad, if desired.

Makes: 6-8 servings

Prep: 10 mins

Cook: 1 hr.

Ingredients:

- 2 cups whole milk
- 5 large eggs
- 1 teaspoon salt
- Freshly ground black pepper
- 8 cups day-old French or Italian bread, roughly torn into 1 ½-inch cubes
- 3 Tablespoons olive oil

- 1 large yellow onion, peeled and diced
- 10 oz. mixed wild mushrooms, trimmed and sliced
- 2 large cloves garlic, peeled and minced
- 1 (10-ounce) package frozen leaf spinach, defrosted and squeezed very dry
- 6 ounces feta cheese, crumbled
- 1 Tablespoon finely chopped fresh thyme leaves
- Nonstick vegetable spray
- ¼ cup grated aged Asiago cheese

Directions:

In a large bowl, beat together the salt, eggs, milk, and black pepper to taste. Stir in the bread cubes, turning to coat evenly, and let them stand until the liquid is absorbed, about 15 minutes.

Meanwhile, preheat the oven to 350°F.

Heat a 10-inch cast-iron skillet over med-high heat until hot. Add the oil and onions and sauté until golden, about 5 minutes. Stir in the mushrooms, and cook until the mushrooms are wilted, stirring or shaking the pan occasionally. Add in the garlic, cook for 1 min, and then stir in the spinach. Gently fold the mushroom mixture, feta cheese, and thyme into the bread cubes.

Wipe out the pan if necessary. Spray the pan with vegetable spray. Put the mixture back into the skillet and bake for 40 minutes. Sprinkle on the Asiago cheese and continue baking until the top is puffed and golden brown, about 10 minutes. Remove from the oven and serve.

28. Ginger-Spice-Topped Peach Cobbler

Cobblers are among the most popular of Southern desserts. In this simple yet personal version, a ginger-spice batter is poured into the pan and topped by peaches. Serve the dessert directly from the skillet with ice cream or whipped cream.

Makes: 8 servings

Prep: 10 mins

Cook: 45 mins

Ingredients:

Filling:

- 3 Tablespoons water
- 2 ½ Tablespoons cornstarch
- 2 (16-ounce) packages frozen peaches, defrosted
- 1 cup sugar
- 2 Tablespoons freshly squeezed lemon juice

Topping:

- 6 Tablespoons unsalted butter
- 1 cup self-rising flour
- ⅓ cup sugar
- ⅓ cup firmly packed light brown sugar
- 1 Teaspoon ground ginger
- ¼ tsp. salt
- ⅛ tsp. ground clove
- 1 cup whole milk
- Vanilla ice cream, to serve
- ½ tsp. of cinnamon

Directions:

Preheat your oven to 350°F. Put a baking sheet in the middle of the oven.

In a large bowl, stir the water and cornstarch until smooth.

Add the peaches, sugar, and lemon juice and stir. Set aside.

In a 10-inch cast-iron skillet, heat the butter over medium heat until melted. Meanwhile, in a med. bowl, mix the flour, white and brown sugars, ginger, cinnamon, salt, and cloves. Whisk the milk and melted butter into the dry ingredients, leaving a thin coating of the butter on the bottom of the skillet.

Reheat the skillet over medium heat; pour in the batter and then add the peaches. Put the skillet on the baking sheet and bake until the cobbler's top is golden brown, about 45 mins. Remove and cool, then serve the cobbler with vanilla ice cream or whipped cream.

29. Raspberry-Blackberry Crisp

A fabulous combination of raspberries and blackberries, this crisp recipe is simple, delicious and absolutely amazing.

Makes: 4-6 servings

Prep: 15 mins

Cook: 40 mins

Ingredients:

- Unsalted butter to grease the skillet
- 1 Tablespoon + 1 teaspoon cornstarch
- 1 Tablespoon freshly squeezed lemon juice
- 4 cups mixed fresh blackberries and raspberries
- ½ to ⅔ cup sugar, depending on how sweet the berries are
- ⅔ cup quick-cooking oatmeal
- ⅓ cup unbleached all-purpose flour
- ⅓ cup firmly packed dark brown sugar
- ⅛ teaspoon salt

- 4 Tablespoons unsalted butter, at room temperature

Vanilla ice cream or sweetened whipped cream

Directions:

Preheat your oven to 375°F. Put a baking sheet in the middle of the oven. Lightly butter a 10-inch cast-iron skillet.

In a large bowl, stir the cornstarch and lemon juice together until blended; add the berries and sugar, and gently stir to combine them evenly. Scrape the mixture into the skillet.

In the same bowl, combine the salt, flour, brown sugar, oatmeal, and butter. Stir the mix until crumbly and blended and scatter it over the berries. Transfer the skillet to the baking sheet in the oven & bake until the topping is set, about 40 minutes. Remove and cool for at least 15 mins before serving the crisp from the skillet with vanilla ice cream or whipped cream.

30. Roast Chicken With Root Vegetables

This recipe ensures that the chicken is golden brown with crisp skin, tender meat, subtle spice, and butteriness.

Makes: 4 servings

Prep: 20 mins

Cook: 1 hr. 5 mins

Ingredients:

- 1 whole chicken, cleaned, at room temperature
- 4 tablespoons salted butter, at room temperature
- 10 garlic cloves, peeled
- Sea salt
- Freshly ground black pepper
- 6 medium carrots, roughly chopped
- 3 beets, purple and golden, roughly chopped
- 3 red potatoes, roughly chopped
- 1 yellow onion, roughly chopped

- ¼ cup olive oil

Directions:

Preheat the oven to 475°F.

Rub the chicken with the butter, taking care to coat the chicken underneath the skin.

Cut 10 small slits in the chicken throughout the body. Fill each slit with 1 garlic clove.

Season with sea salt and black pepper.

In a cast iron Dutch oven, put the carrots, beets, potatoes, and onion.

Add the olive oil, season with sea salt and black pepper, and toss to coat.

Make a bed in the vegetables and nestle the chicken on top.

Roast, uncovered, for 20 mins. Lower the oven temp to 400°F and continue to roast, uncovered, for 45 minutes.

Let the chicken cool slightly before serving.

Conclusion

You've reached the end! Make sure to try out all 30 of these simple yet delicious cast iron recipes and don't forget to share with your friends and family.

Part 2

Recipe 1: Simple Cheesy Omelet

This is a cheesy omelet that you can enjoy anytime that you wish. Feel free to add any kind of vegetables you want to make this dish incredibly healthy.

Yield: 2 Servings

Preparation Time: **15 Minutes**

List of Ingredients:

- 6 Tablespoon of Butter, Unsalted Variety and Evenly Divided
- 1 Zucchini, Large in Size and Sliced Thinly
- 1 Onion, Medium in Size and Sliced Thinly
- Dash of Salt and Pepper, For Taste
- 1 Clove of Garlic, Minced
- 2 teaspoons of Marjoram Leaves, Fresh
- ½ Cup of Fontina Cheese, Freshly Grated
- 6 Eggs, Large in Size and Beaten Lightly
- 1 Tablespoon of Parsley, Flat Leaf Variety, Fresh and Roughly Chopped
- Some Mixed Greens, For Serving

Instructions:

1. The first thing that you will want to do is heat up some butter in a large sized cast iron skillet placed over medium to high heat. Once the butter is melted add in

your squash and onions and cook until soft to the touch. This should take at least 8 to 10 minutes. Season with some salt and pepper.

2. Then add in your garlic and marjoram. Continue to cook for at least one minute. Remove and transfer to a plate.

3. Wipe your skillet clean and add in some more butter. Place over medium heat and add in your eggs. Cook and swirl gently until your eggs are set and the bottom of the eggs are gold in color.

4. Top your omelet with half of your veggies mixture and half of your cheese. Fold over gently and slide onto a plate.

5. Repeat until all of your ingredients are used up and serve with your parsley and greens. Enjoy!

Recipe 2: Cast Iron Style Chicken Piccata

Here is a filling cast iron dish that I know you and your entire family will fall in love with. Feel free to serve this dish with whatever side you wish to make it truly delicious.

Yield: 4 Servings

Preparation Time: **30 Minutes**

List of Ingredients:

- 4, 6 Ounce Chicken Cutlets
- ½ Cup of Flour, All Purpose Variety
- 1 ½ teaspoon of Salt, For Taste
- ¼ teaspoon of Black Pepper, For Taste
- 1 Egg, Large in Size, White Only and Beaten Lightly
- 6 Tablespoon of Butter, Salted Variety and Evenly Divided
- 2 tablespoons of Olive Oil, Evenly Divided
- 1 Cup of Chicken Broth, Low in Sodium
- ¼ Cup of Lemon Juice, Fresh
- 2 tablespoons of Capers, Brined Variety, Drained and Rinsed
- 1/3 Cup of Parsley, Flat Leaf Variety and Roughly Chopped
- Some Pasta, Hot and Fully Cooked

Instructions:

1. First place each of your chicken cutlets between two pieces of plastic wrap and flatten with a meat mallet until at least a quarter inch in thickness.

2. The stir together your flour, salt and pepper until thoroughly combined. Then dip your chicken into your egg white and dredge in your flour mixture, making sure to shake off the excess flour.

3. Next melt your butter and olive oil together in a large sized cast iron skillet placed over medium to high heat. Once hot enough add in your chicken cutlets and cook for at least 2 to 3 minutes on both sides. Remove from your skillet and set aside.

4. Then add in your broth, lemon juice and capers to your cast iron skillet and bring this mixture to a boil over high heat, making sure to stir thoroughly.

5. Next reduce the heat to low and whisk for the next 5 minutes. Add in your remaining ingredients and whisk thoroughly to combine. Spoon this sauce over your chicken and serve immediately and enjoy.

Recipe 3: Cast Iron Skillet Baked Chocolate Chip Cookie

One of the best treats to enjoy during a snowy day is this giant cast iron skillet style cookie. Serve this with a large glass of milk to make it a dessert dish you will want to make over and over again.

Yield: 4 Servings

Preparation Time: **1 Hour**

List of Ingredients:

- 2 Cups of Flour, All Purpose Variety
- 1 teaspoon of Baker's Style Baking Soda
- ½ teaspoon of Salt, For Taste
- ¾ Cup of Butter, Unsalted Variety and Soft
- ½ Cup of Sugar, Granulated Variety
- ¾ Cup of Brown Sugar, Light and Packed
- 1 Egg, Large in Size and Beaten Lightly
- 2 teaspoons of Vanilla, Pure
- 1 ½ Cups of Chocolate Chips, Your Favorite Kind

Instructions:

1. First preheat your oven to 350 degrees.
2. While your oven is heating up mix together your first three ingredients until thoroughly combined. Set aside.

3. Then use an electric mixture and cream together your butter and your sugar until light and fluffy in consistency. This should take about two minutes. Then add in your egg and vanilla and mix thoroughly again to fully mix.

4. Add this to your flour mixture and beat with your electric mixture until thoroughly combined. Slowly and gently fold in your chocolate chips and transfer mixture to a large sized cast iron skillet.

5. Place into your oven at to bake for the next 40 to 45 minutes or until the top is golden brown in color. Remove and allow to cool slightly before serving.

Recipe 4: Spicy Cast Iron Salsa

With the help of this dish you can turn your cast iron skillet into a Mexican dream. This dish uses charred onions, charred garlic and spicy peppers to make a salsa recipe that you won't be able to resist.

Yield: 2 Servings

Preparation Time: **30 Minutes**

List of Ingredients:

- 3 Tomatoes, Plum Variety and Cut into Halves
- 3 Cloves of Garlic, Unpeeled
- 1 Jalapeno Pepper, Green in Color and Cut into Halves
- 1 Onion, White in Color, Medium in Size and Cut into Wedges
- 1 ½ Tablespoon of Lime Juice, Fresh
- ¾ teaspoon of Salt, For Taste
- 1/3 Cup of Cilantro Leaves, Fresh and Roughly Chopped

Instructions:

1. The first thing that you want to do is heat up your cast iron skillet over medium heat for at least five minutes. After that add in your tomatoes, garlic and jalapeno peppers. Stir thoroughly for the next 6 minutes or until thoroughly charred and soft to the touch.

2. Transfer this mixture to a food processor and blend until thoroughly pulsed. Add in your garlic next to your blender and pulse again.

3. Add your onions to your skillet and cook for at least 5 to 6 minutes or until charred and soft on both sides. Transfer to a blender and pulse again.

4. Continue to pulse your salsa until it reaches the desired consistency. Pour into a bowl and stir in your cilantro. Serve whenever you are ready and enjoy.

Recipe 5: Indoor Style S'mores

Whoever said s'mores could only be made outside? Well, with the help of this recipe you can make this tasty treat whenever you want. I know your kids are going to love this dish.

Yield: 2 Servings

Preparation Time: **11 Minutes**

List of Ingredients:

- 1 Cup of Chocolate Chips, Your Favorite Kind
- 8 Marshmallows, Large in Size
- Some Graham Crackers, For Dipping

Instructions:

1. First preheat your oven to 450 degrees.
2. While your oven is heating up is a large sized cast iron skillet and add in your chocolate chips.
3. Cut your marshmallows in half and top your chocolate chips with them.
4. Place into your oven to bake the next 7 to 9 minutes or until your marshmallows are golden brown in color.
5. Remove from your oven and serve with your Graham crackers whenever you are ready.

Recipe 6: Ginger And Peach Shortbread Cobbler

Here is a great tasting dessert dish that the entire family will love. IT is the perfect dessert dish to make when you want to make a dessert dish to end your dinner meal on a sweet note.

Yield: 6 to 8 Servings
Preparation Time: 1 Hour and 10 Minutes

List of Ingredients:

- 1 Cup of Butter, Soft
- ½ Cup of Brown Sugar, Light and Packed
- 1/8 teaspoon of Salt, For Taste
- 2 ¼ Cups + 3 tablespoons of Flour, All Purpose Variety and Evenly Divided
- 1 Pieces of Ginger, Fresh and Peeled
- ¾ Cup of Sugar, Turbinado Variety and Evenly Divided
- 7 to 9 Peaches, Medium in Size and Cut into Halves
- 2 tablespoons of Lemon Juice, Freshly Squeezed
- 1 Egg, Large in Size, White Only and Beaten Lightly
- 2 teaspoons of Sugar

Instructions:

1. First you want to preheat your oven to 400 degrees.

2. While your oven is heating up mix your first three ingredients together as well as your flour using an electric mixer until thoroughly combined.

3. Then place your dough onto a lightly floured surface and roll until at least quarter inch in thickness. Cut out at least 14 discs from your dough and place into a single layer on it generously greased baking sheet.

4. Next place your ginger and sugar together in a food processor and pulse for at least 5 to 6 times or until thoroughly chopped and combined. Pour this mixture into a bowl and add any remaining sugar and stir thoroughly to combine. Add in your next 3 ingredients and toss thoroughly to coat.

5. Place this mixture into a cast iron skillet and pour any remaining juice over your peaches.

6. Place into your oven to bake for the next 15 minutes. After this time remove and brush your rounds with your egg whites. Sprinkle with some sugar and placed back into oven to bake for another 17 to 20 minutes

7. After this time remove from the oven and allow to cool slightly before serving.

Recipe 7: Sweet Tasting Blueberry Cobbler

Here is yet another great tasting dessert dish that I know you are going to want to make as often as possible. This is perfect to make if you are a huge fan of traditional blueberry pie and are looking for something more on the festive side.

Yield: 4 Servings

Preparation Time: **35 Minutes**

List of Ingredients:

- 1 Cup + 2 tablespoons of Flour, All Purpose Variety
- ¾ Cup + 3 tablespoons of Sugar
- 1 ¼ teaspoon of Baker's Style Baking Powder
- 3 tablespoons of Butter, Unsalted and Cut into Small Cubes
- 1 Egg, Large in Size and Beaten Lightly
- ¼ Cup of Cream, Heavy Variety
- 5 Cups of Blueberries, Fresh
- ¾ teaspoon of Orange Zest, Freshly Grated
- ¼ teaspoon of Mace, Ground Variety
- 2/3 Cup of Orange Juice, Freshly Squeezed
- Some Ice Cream, Your Favorite Kind and for Serving

Instructions:

1. First use a medium sized bowl and combine at least one cup of your flour with 3 tablespoons of sugar. Add

in your baking powder and butter and stir thoroughly until crumbly.

2. Then add in your egg and cream and mix again to combine. Your mixture should form a soft dough.

3. Use a large cast iron skillet and combine your remaining sugar, flour, orange zest, mace and blueberries together until thoroughly combined.

4. Pour in your orange juice and cook your mixture over medium to low heat. Allow to come to a boil before reducing the heat to low. Allow to cook for at least 2 minutes or until thick in consistency. Remove your skillet from heat.

5. Drop some of your biscuits by the tablespoon onto your fruit until you have at least 12 to 16 biscuits.

6. Place into your oven to bake for the next 16 minutes or until lightly brown on the top. Remove from the oven and allow to cool slightly before serving.

Recipe 8: Sweet Tasting Potato And Green Onion Cakes

These savory little cakes make for the perfect appetizer to serve during your next dinner gathering. For the tastiest results I highly recommend serving these with a small dollop of sour cream and a light squeeze of some lime juice.

Yield: 6 to 8 Servings
Preparation Time: 1 Hour and 5 Minutes

List of Ingredients:

- 4 Sweet Potatoes, Medium in Size
- 2 Eggs, Lightly Beaten
- ½ Cup of Flour, All Purpose Variety
- 2 Jalapeno Peppers, Red in Color and Finely Chopped
- 1 ½ teaspoon of Salt, For Taste
- ½ Cup of Green Onion, Sliced Thinly and Evenly Divided
- ¼ Cup of Oil, Canola Variety
- Some Lime Wedges, For Garnish

Instructions:

1. First pierce the potatoes several times using a fork and place into a microwave-safe plate. Cover potatoes with some damn paper towels and microwave on high

for the next 8 to 10 minutes or until your potatoes are tender to the touch. After this time allow to stand for at least five minutes before peeling and grating.

2. Stir together your grated mashed potatoes with your eggs and next 3 ingredients. Add in your green onions and stir thoroughly to combine.

3. Pour some oil into a large sized cast iron skillet and heat over medium to high heat. Drop your mixture by the tablespoon into your hot oil and press lately with a spatula to flatten. Fry for the next 5 to 6 minutes on each side or until golden brown in color. After this time remove from your oil and drain on a plate line with paper towels.

4. Repeat until all of your mixture has been used and serve with some green onions. Enjoy.

Recipe 9: Classic Artichoke And Kale Dip

This is the perfect dish that you can make to help rein in the holiday season. It is light, sweet and delicious when made with fresh chips. Make this as a tasty appetizer dish to satisfy the taste buds of your family.

Yield: 4 to 6 Servings

Preparation Time: **25 Minutes**

List of Ingredients:

- 2 tablespoons of Olive Oil, Extra Virgin Variety
- ½ an Onion, Yellow in Color, Medium in Size and Finely Diced
- 2 Cloves of Garlic, Minced
- 1 Bunch of Kale, Stems Removed and Roughly Chopped
- 1, 8 Ounce Pack of Artichoke Hearts, Thawed
- 8 Ounces of Cream Cheese, Soft
- ½ Cup of Mayonnaise, Your Favorite Kind
- 1 Cup of Pepper Jack Cheese
- ¼ teaspoon of Salt, For Taste
- ¼ teaspoon of Black Pepper, For Taste
- 1 ½ Cups of Potato Chips, Finely Crushed
- Some Bread, For Dipping

Instructions:

1. The first thing that you want to do you preheat your oven to 375 degrees.
2. Then use a large cast iron skillet and heat up your oil over medium heat. Once the oil is hot enough add in your onions and garlic and cook for the next 30 seconds.
3. Add in your kale and cook just until it begins to wilt before adding in your artichoke hearts. Stir thoroughly to combine and continue cooking until your kale is soft to the touch.
4. Then use a medium sized bowl and mix together your cream cheese, pepper jack cheese, dash of salt and pepper and your favorite kind of mayonnaise until thoroughly combined. Pour this into your kale mixture and stir well until thoroughly coated.
5. Top with your potato chips and place into your oven to bake for the next 15 minutes or until the top is brown in color. Remove and allow to cool slightly before serving. Enjoy.

Recipe 10: Tasty Chicken And Wild Rice

This simple one pot meal is the perfect dish to make when you find yourself tight on time. This dish is held beautifully by some tangy gravy and serve with some wild rice, making it not only incredibly delicious, but incredibly easy to make.

Yield: 4 Servings
Preparation Time: 1 Hour and 40 Minutes

List of Ingredients:

- 1 ¼ teaspoon of Salt, Evenly Divided
- 1, 6 Ounce Pack of Rice, Wild Variety and Uncooked
- 3 tablespoons of Butter, Soft
- 1/3 Cup of Flour, All Purpose Variety
- 1 Cup of Milk, Whole
- 2 ½ Cups of Chicken Broth
- 1 ½ teaspoon of Mustard, Dry Variety
- ¾ teaspoon of Black Pepper, For Taste and Evenly Divided
- ½ Cup of Ham, Country Variety and Finely Chopped
- 2 tablespoons of Olive Oil, Extra Virgin Variety and Evenly Divided
- 1 Cup of Onion, Yellow in Color and Finely Chopped
- 8 Ounces of Mushrooms, Fresh, Assorted Variety and Finely Chopped

- 3 Cloves of Garlic, Finely Chopped
- 2 tablespoons of Wine, White in Color and Your Favorite Kind
- 4 Chicken Breasts, Skinned and Bone in Variety
- Some Parsley, For Garnish
- Some Almonds, Finely Sliced, For Garnish and Optional

Instructions:

1. The first thing that you want to do is bring some salt and water to boil in a large sized saucepan. Stir in your rice and allow to boil before reducing the heat to low. Cover and cook for the next 30 minutes until your rice is tender to the touch.

2. While your rice is cooking melt your butter in a large sized cast iron skillet placed over low heat. Add in your flour and whisk thoroughly until smooth in consistency. Then add in your milk and next 2 ingredients before increasing the heat to medium. Continue to cook for the next 3 to 4 minutes or until your mixture is thick in consistency. Season with a dash of salt and pepper and set aside.

3. Use another cast iron skillet and heat up some oil over medium to high heat. Once the oil is hot enough add in your ham and cook for the next 6 minutes or until light brown in color. Then add in your onions and next 2 ingredients, making sure to stir thoroughly for the next 6 minutes.

4. Add in your garlic and cook for at least one minute before adding in your wine. Continue to cook until your wine is for evaporated.

5. Then preheat your oven to 375 degrees.

6. While your oven is heating up season your chicken with some salt and pepper and heat up some oil in your cast iron skillet. Once your oil is hot enough cook your chicken until thoroughly brown in color. Remove from your skillet and set aside for later use.

7. Next stir together your cooked rice, ham mixture and sauce in a large sized cast iron skillet and place your chicken on top

8. Place into your oven to bake for the next 30 minutes or until your chicken is fully done and your mixture is bubbly. Remove and allow to stand for at least 10 minutes before serving. Enjoy.

Recipe 11: Four Cheese Rigatoni

Here is yet another dish you can make if you are looking to enjoy some authentic comfort food. I guarantee that once they get a taste of it, even the pickiest of eaters won't be able to resist this dish.

Yield: 4 to 6 Servings

Preparation Time: **50 Minutes**

List of Ingredients:

- 1 Pound of Rigatoni, Mini Variety
- 1 Shallot, Fresh and Finely Sliced
- 2 Cloves of Garlic, Minced
- ½ teaspoon of Olive Oil, Extra Virgin Variety
- 5 Tablespoon of Butter, Soft and Unsalted Variety
- ¼ Cup of Flour, All Purpose Variety
- 2 Cups of Milk, Whole
- 1/3 Cup of Cheese, Mascarpone Variety
- 8 Ounces of Gruyere Cheese, Freshly Grated
- 8 Ounces of Cheddar Cheese, Sharp and Freshly Grated
- 8 Ounces of Fontina Cheese, Freshly Grated
- ¼ teaspoon of Salt, For Taste
- ½ teaspoon of Pepper, For Taste
- ¼ teaspoon of Nutmeg, Ground Variety

- 1/3 Cup of Breadcrumbs, Panko Variety

Instructions:

1. The first thing that you will want to do is preheat your oven to 375 degrees.
2. While your oven is heat up grate your cheeses and place them into a large sized bowl.
3. Next boil some water over medium to high heat and cook your pasta according to the directions on the package until tender to the touch. After this time remove, drain and set aside.
4. Then heat up a large sized cast iron skillet and add in your oil. Once your oil is hot enough add in your shallots with some salt. Cook for the next 3 minutes or until soft to the touch.
5. Add in your garlic and continue to cook for an additional 30 seconds before adding in your flour. Cook until a roux begins to form and turns golden brown in color.
6. Pour in your milk and continuously stir for the next 1 to 2 minutes. Add in your mascarpone and most of your freshly grated cheeses. Stir continuously until your mixture is thick in consistency. This should take at least 3 to 4 minutes.
7. Season with some extra salt, pepper and ground nutmeg. Feel free to add more if your need to.
8. Then add in your pasta and toss thoroughly to coat.
9. Top your mixture with your remaining cheese and breadcrumbs.

10. Place into your oven to bake for the next 30 to 35 minutes or until the top of your mixture is golden brown in color and is bubbly.

11. After this time remove from your oven and serve while it is still piping hot. Enjoy.

Recipe 12: Cast Iron Mac And Cheese

If you love the taste of mac and cheese, then I know you are certainly going to fall in love with this recipe. I guarantee the moment you serve this dish to your family it will soon become a favorite in your household.

Yield: 6 Servings

Preparation Time: **45 Minutes**

List of Ingredients:

- 1/2 of 16 Ounce Pack of Pasta, Cellentani Variety
- 2 tablespoons of Butter, Soft
- 1 Onion, Medium in Size and Finely Diced
- 1 Green Bell Pepper, Finely Diced
- 1, 10 Ounce Can of Tomatoes and Green Chiles, Finely Diced
- 1, 8 Ounce Pack of Cheese, Your Favorite Kind and Cubed
- 3 Cups of Chicken, Fully Cooked and Finely Chopped
- 1, 10.2 Ounce Can of Cream of Chicken Soup, Your Favorite Kind
- ½ Cup of Sour Cream
- 1 teaspoon of Chili, Powdered Variety
- ½ teaspoon of Cumin, Ground
- 1 ½ Cups of Cheddar Cheese, Finely Shredded

Instructions:

1. First preheat your oven to 350 degrees.
2. While your oven is heating up prepare your pasta according to the directions on the package.
3. Next melt your butter in a large sized cast iron skillet placed over medium to high heat. Once it is melted add in your onions and peppers and cook for the next 5 minutes until they are tender to the touch.
4. Then add in your tomatoes and next 2 ingredients, making sure to stir thoroughly for the next 2 minutes until your cheese melts completely.
5. Next add in your chicken along with your next 4 ingredients and your hot pasta and stir thoroughly until blended together.
6. Remove from heat and transfer it to your oven to bake for the next 25 to 30 minutes or until bubbly. After this time remove and allow to cool slightly before serving. Enjoy.

Recipe 13: Tasty Blue Cheese And Beet Risotto

This is a great tasting dish to make when root vegetables begin to come into season. This dish is incredibly sweet and compliments practically anything that you make with it.

Yield: 4 Servings
Preparation Time: 1 Hour and 40 Minutes

List of Ingredients:

- ¾ Pound of Beets, Golden in Color
- Dash of Salt and Pepper, For Taste
- 5 Cups of Chicken Broth, Low in Sodium
- 3 tablespoons of Butter, Unsalted and Soft
- 1 Onion, Yellow in Color, Small in Size and Chopped Finely
- 1 ½ Cups of Rice, Arborio Variety
- ½ Cup of Wine, White in Color
- 1/3 Cup of Parmesan Cheese, Freshly Grated
- ¼ Cup of Blue Cheese, Crumbled

Instructions:

1. The first thing that you want to do is preheat your oven to 400 degrees.

2. While your oven is heating up place your beets into a baking dish and cover with some water. Cover with aluminum foil and bake in your oven until your beets

are tender to the touch. I should take at least 40 minutes to 1 hour. After this time uncover and allow to cool before chopping finely. Season with some salt.

3. Next use a large sized saucepan and bring your broth to a simmer over medium heat.

4. Then use a large sized cast iron skillet and heat up your butter over medium heat. Once the butter is melted add in your onions and salt and cook until onions are soft. Then add in your rice and cook until translucent.

5. Add in your wine and continue to cook until your wine has been fully absorbed. Add in a little of your broth and continue cooking while simmering until all of your liquid has been absorbed. Repeat until the broth has been absorbed again. This should take at least 25 minutes in total.

6. Then add in your tender beets and cook for an additional minute.

7. Add in your remaining butter and cheese. Remove from heat.

8. Allow to sit for at least 2 minutes and season with some salt and pepper if you desire. Serve and enjoy.

Recipe 14: Cast Iron Filet Mignon

If you have never had the delicious taste of Filet mignon, you really need to give this recipe a try for yourself. Filet Mignon is absolutely delicious and makes for the perfect dish to make whenever you are looking to make something on the fancier side.

Yield: 4 Servings

Preparation Time: **4 Servings**

List of Ingredients:

- 4, 6 Ounce of Beef Fillets, Tenderloin Variety
- 1 teaspoon of Pepper, For Taste
- ½ teaspoon of Salt, For Taste
- 2 tablespoons of Butter, Soft
- 2 tablespoons of Olive Oil, Extra Virgin Variety

Instructions:

1. The first thing that you would want to do is sprinkle your fillets with a generous amount of salt and pepper.
2. Then melt your butter and olive oil together in a large skillet placed over medium heat.
3. Once melted add in your fish fillets and cook for the next 5 to 7 minutes on each side or until it is done to your desired likeness.
4. After this time remove and allow to sit for at least 5 minutes before serving.

Recipe 15: Cast Iron Bbq Style Pizza

Here is a personal favorite recipe of mine and once you make it for yourself, I know it will become a favorite of yours too.

Yield: 6 to 8 Servings

Preparation Time: 2 Hours and 30 Minutes

Ingredients for Your Pizza Dough:

- 3 ¾ Cup of Flour, Bread Variety
- 2 ½ teaspoon of Yeast, Active and Dry Variety
- ¾ teaspoon of Salt, For Taste
- ¾ teaspoon of Sugar
- 1 1/3 Cups of Water, Room Temperature

Ingredients for Your Pizza:

- ¼ Cup of Pizza Sauce, Your Favorite Kind
- ¼ Cup of BBQ Sauce, Your Favorite Kind
- 1 ½ Cups of Mozzarella Cheese, Finely Shredded
- ½ of a Jalapeno Pepper, Sliced Thinly
- 1 Cup of BBQ Ribs, Finely Chopped
- 1 Tablespoon of Butter, Unsalted Variety

Instructions:

1. First use a small sized bowl and combine your yeast and warm water together until your yeast fully dissolves.

2. Then use a food processor and thoroughly combine your flour, sugar and salt. Pulse to blend together and then add in your water and yeast mixture. Pulse again until a dough begins to form.
3. Cover your dough with some plastic wrap and allow to rise in a warm area for at least an hour.
4. Then preheat your oven to broil. Place your cast iron skillets into your oven to heat up.
5. After one hour place your dough ball onto a lightly floured surface and roll into a small circle. Place into your cast iron skillet.
6. Top your dough with your pizza toppings in whatever order you desire.
7. Place into your oven to boil for at least 45 seconds before rotating it and broiling for another minute and a half. Continue to broil until your cheese is bubbly and your crust begins to char. Remove and serve while still piping hot.

Recipe 16: Pecan Okra

If you are looking for a delicious yet healthy appetizer dish to serve, then this is the perfect dish for you. Easy to make and ready in just a couple of minutes, I know you and your guests are going to fall in love with this dish.

Yield: 6 to 8 Servings

Preparation Time: **25 Minutes**

List of Ingredients:

- 1 Cup of Pecans, Finely Crushed
- 1 ½ Cup of Bisquick, Dried
- 1 teaspoon of Salt, For Taste
- ½ teaspoon of Pepper, For Taste
- 2, 10 Ounce Packs of Okra, Whole
- Some Oil, Vegetable Variety or Peanut Variety, For Frying

Instructions:

1. The first thing that you want to do this place your pecans in a single layer in a cast iron skillet.
2. Then place into your oven to bake at 350 degrees for at least 10 minutes or until lightly toasted. Make sure that you stir your nuts occasionally.
3. Next use a food processor and combine your Bisquick, toasted nuts and next 2 ingredients until finely ground.

4. Place your ground pecan mixture into a large sized bowl before adding in your okra. Once your okra has been added, toss thoroughly to coat

5. Next pour your oil into a large sized cast iron skillet and heat over medium to high heat. Once it is hot enough fry your okra for at least 5 to 6 minutes or until golden in color. Remove and drain on a plate lined with paper towels.

6. Repeat until all of your okra has been fried and served whenever you are ready. Enjoy.

Recipe 17: Lamb Chops In Garlic Mint Sauce

Here is another great tasting cast iron skillet meal that I know you are going to love. For the tastiest results I highly recommend serving this dish with some mashed potatoes to make a filling meal that you will want to make over and over again.

Yield: 4 Servings

Preparation Time: **40 Minutes**

List of Ingredients:

- 12 Lamb Chops
- Dash of Salt, For Taste
- ½ Cup of Mint Leaves, Fresh and Roughly Chopped
- 1 Tablespoon of Garlic, Finely Chopped
- ¼ Cup of Vinegar, Balsamic Variety
- ¼ Cup + 1 Tablespoon of Olive Oil, Extra Virgin Variety
- 1 Head of Cauliflower, Cut into Small Sized Florets
- 1 Tablespoon of Butter, Unsalted Variety and Soft
- ½ Cup of Cream, Heavy Variety
- Dash of Black Pepper, For Taste

Instructions:

1. The first thing that you would want to do is season your lamb on both sides with a generous amount of salt. Set aside for later use.
2. Then use a small sized bowl and combine your next 4 ingredients together. Add in your oil and stir until thick in consistency. Set aside for later use.
3. Next bring some water to a boil in a medium sized saucepan placed over medium heat. Add in your florets into a steamer basket and set to steam until your cauliflower is tender to the touch. This should take at least 8 to 10 minutes.
4. Then melt your butter in a large sized cast iron skillet and add in your cauliflower. Mash until thoroughly mashed and then add in your cream. Heat over low heat for the next two to three minutes before seasoning with salt and pepper.
5. Serve with their lamb chops and some sauce. Enjoy.

Recipe 18: Simple Cowboy Style Steak

If you are a huge fan of steak, then I know this is going to be one recipe you are going to love. With the help of this dish you don't have to worry about smoking up your house. Instead you can enjoy restaurant style steak anytime you wish.

Yield: 2 to 4 Servings

Preparation Time: **1 Hour**

List of Ingredients:

- Dash of Salt and Pepper, For Taste
- 1, 2 Pound Rib Eye Steak, Bone in Variety
- 1 Tablespoon of Oil, Vegetable Variety
- 3 tablespoons of Butter, Soft
- 8 Sprigs of Thyme, Rosemary and Oregano, Fresh
- 3 Cloves of Garlic, Peeled and Smashed

Instructions:

1. The first thing that you will want to do is preheat an indoor grill to at least 400 to 450 degrees. Place your cast iron skillet on your grill and allow to heat up for the next 15 minutes.

2. While your skillet is heating up season your steak with a generous amount of salt and pepper.

3. Then add some oil to your skillet and place your steak onto your skillet. Grill for at least 10 minutes or until dark brown and crusty. Flip and continue grilling

for at least 10 minutes or until done to your desired likeness.

4. While your steak is grilling, add in your remaining ingredients to your skillet and cook for at least 2 to 3 minutes or until your butter begins to Bubble. Pour this mixture over your steak and serve whenever you are ready. Enjoy.

Recipe 19: Easy Egg And Sweet Potato Skillet

Sometimes simple dishes are always the best dishes. The same holds true with this delicious dish. The best part about this dish is that it is a great dish for vegetarians and vegans to enjoy as well.

Yield: 2 to 3 Servings

Preparation Time: **15 Minutes**

List of Ingredients:

- 1 Sweet Potato, Large in Size
- 4 Eggs, Large in Size
- ½ Cup of Mozzarella Cheese, Finely Shredded
- ½ teaspoon of Paprika, Smoke Variety
- Dash of Salt and Pepper, For Taste

Instructions:

1. The first thing that you will want to do is pierce your sweet potatoes with a fork and place into your microwave. Cook for at least 8 minutes or until your sweet potatoes are tender.
2. While your potatoes are cooking preheat your broiler.
3. Next slice your sweet potato into rounds and place into a cast iron skillet.
4. Crack your eggs over your potatoes and season with some salt and pepper. Season with paprika and top with your cheese.

5. Place into your oven to broil for at least 3 minutes or until your eggs are completely set. Remove and serve whenever you are ready.

Recipe 20: Simple Cast Iron Lasagna

This is the perfect recipe to make if you have people in your family that are huge fans of lasagna. All that you need for this recipes if one skillet to make a truly delicious meal you won't be able to resist.

Yield: 6 Servings

Preparation Time: **45 Minutes**

List of Ingredients:

- 1, 28 Ounce Can of Tomatoes, Crushed
- 1, 8 Ounce Can of Tomato Sauce
- ¼ Cup of Water, Warm
- 1 Tablespoon of Olive Oil, Extra Virgin Variety
- 1 Onion, Yellow in Color, Medium in Size and Finely Diced
- 4 Cloves of Garlic, Minced
- ½ teaspoon of Salt, For Taste
- ¼ teaspoon of Black Pepper, For Taste
- ¼ teaspoon of Red Pepper Flakes, Crushed
- ¾ Pound of Chuck, Lean and Ground
- ¼ Pound of Sausage, Italian Variety
- 8 Lasagna Noodles, Whole and Broken into Small Pieces
- ½ Cup of Ricotta Cheese

- 4 Ounces of Mozzarella, Fresh and Sliced Thinly
- Some Basil Leaves, Fresh and Roughly Torn
- Some Parmesan Cheese, Shaved and for Garnish

Instructions:

1. Use a large sized bowl and add in your tomatoes, tomato sauce and water. Stir thoroughly to combine.
2. Then heat up a large sized skillet over medium heat and add in your olive oil. Once your oil is hot enough add in your onions and cook until they are soft. Then add in your garlic and continue to cook for 1 minute before adding in here next 3 ingredients. Cook for an additional 30 seconds.
3. Then add in your next 2 ingredients and cook until thoroughly browned in color.
4. Then place your lasagna noodles on top of your beef and sausage mixture. Pour your tomato sauce over the top and bring this mixture to a simmer over low heat.
5. Cook until your noodles are tender to the touch and then stir everything together. Drop your ricotta cheese by the spoonful and stir thoroughly to combine.
6. Top with their mozzarella cheese and cook for an additional 5 minutes before removing from heat and serving.

Recipe 21: Simple Cast Iron Fried Chicken

If you are a huge fan of authentic fried chicken, then this is the perfect dish for you to make. It is easy and pairs excellently with a side of mashed potatoes and fresh veggies.

Yield: 4 Servings

Preparation Time: **40 Minutes**

List of Ingredients:

- ¼ Cup of Brown Sugar, Light and Packed
- 3 tablespoons of Worcestershire Sauce
- 1 Tablespoon of Tabasco Sauce
- Dash of Salt and Pepper, For Taste
- 4 Chicken Thighs, Boneless Variety
- 4 Chicken Drumsticks, Bone-in
- 1 ¼ Cups of Flour, All Purpose Variety
- 2 teaspoons of Cayenne
- 2 teaspoons of Garlic, Powdered Variety
- 2 teaspoons of Baker's Style Baking Powdered
- 2 teaspoons of Paprika, Ground
- 1 Egg, Large in Size and Beaten Lightly
- 3 Cups + 1 Tablespoon of Oil, Vegetable Variety

Instructions:

1. Use a medium-sized saucepan and bring together your first 6 ingredients over medium to high heat. Stir thoroughly until your sugar dissolves and transfer to a bowl. Allow to cool completely.
2. Once cooled add your chicken to the bowl. Place in your fridge for at least 3 hours. After this time pat dry your chicken and set aside
3. Then use another medium sized bowl and whisk together your dry ingredients. Season with salt and pepper and then add in your water, eggs and oil. Stir thoroughly to combine.
4. Next use a large cast iron skillet and heat up your oil over medium to high heat.
5. While your oil is heating up dip each piece of your chicken in your batter, making sure to let the excess run off and then add to your skillet. Fry thoroughly until your chicken is a deep golden brown color. This should take at least 12 to 14 minutes.
6. Once thoroughly fried set aside to drain on a plate line with paper towels and repeat until all of your chicken has been cooked. Serve whenever you are ready.

Recipe 22: Simple Cast Iron Pizza

If you have people in your family that are huge fans of pizza, then this is the perfect dish for you to make. Feel free to add whatever ingredients you want to this dish to make it truly unique and delicious.

Yield: 6 to 8 Servings

Preparation Time: 1 Hour and 10 Minutes

Ingredients for Your Dough:

- 1 ¼ teaspoon of Yeast, Active and Dry
- 1 Cup of Water, Warm
- 2 ¾ Cup of Flour, All Purpose Variety
- 1 ½ teaspoon of Salt, For Taste
- 2 teaspoons of Sugar

Ingredients for Your Toppings:

- ¾ Cup of Pizza Sauce
- 1 Cup of Onions, Caramelized Variety
- Dash of Red Pepper Flakes, Crushed
- 2 Cups of Mozzarella Cheese, Finely Shredded
- 3 Ounces of Prosciutto, Thinly Sliced
- 2 Cups of Arugula, Fresh

Instructions:

1. First use a small sized bowl and combine your yeast and warm water together until your yeast fully dissolves.
2. Then use a food processor and thoroughly combine your flour, sugar and salt. Pulse to blend together and then add in your water and yeast mixture. Pulse again until a dough begins to form.
3. Divide your dough into two equal sized balls and transfer to greased bowl. Cover with some plastic wrap and allow to rise in a warm area for at least an hour.
4. Then preheat your oven to broil. Place your cast iron skillets into your oven to heat up.
5. After one hour place your dough balls onto a lightly floured surface and roll into a small circle. Place into your cast iron skillets.
6. Top your dough with your pizza toppings in whatever order you desire.
7. Place into your oven to boil for at least 45 seconds before rotating it and broiling for another minute and a half. Continue to broil until your cheese is bubbly and your crust begins to char. Remove and serve while still piping hot.

www.ingramcontent.com/pod-product-compliance
Lightning Source LLC
Chambersburg PA
CBHW071459070526
44578CB00001B/391